RAWDON CROZIER

IN AN AGE OF DWARF HOLLYHOCKS

A COLLECTION OF POLITICAL POETRY

Title from "The Dwarf Hollyhock" page 77

Cover Illustration: Rawdon Crozier

COPYRIGHT © 2010 RAWDON CROZIER
All rights reserved. No reproduction, copy or transmission of this publication may be made without written permission or licence, save to the extent and for the purposes permitted by domestic law. The author has asserted his right to be identified as author of this work in accordance with the Copyright, Designs and Patents Act 1988. Any person who does any unauthorised act in relation to this publication may be liable to criminal prosecution and/or civil claims for damages.

First Edition Published 2008 by R R C Crozier, 3 Alton Terrace, Plymouth, PL4 8JY
Second Edition Published 2010 by R R C Crozier, 3 Alton Terrace, Plymouth, PL4 8JY

ISBN 978-0-9561580-0-0

This book is sold subject to the condition that it shall not be given, lent, re-sold, hired out or otherwise circulated without the publisher's prior consent in any form of binding or cover other than that in which it was published, nor without a similar condition (including this condition) being imposed on any subsequent transferee.

CONTENTS

Foreword		5
Introduction to the Political Poetry Section of the Second Edition of 'Collected Poetry'	2008/2010	5
Introduction to the Political Poetry Section of the First Edition of 'Collected Poetry'	2006	12
On the resignation of Harold Wilson	1978	26
On the resignation of Cecil Parkinson	1985	26
On Journalism	1979-91	27
Anger	1993	30
The Tyranny of Nostalgia	1993	31
Questions	1993	32
On a Tree Dying in the Strand	2003	33
Obituary	2004-05	34
The Spin Doctor's Daughter	2005	41
The Politics of Fear	2005	43
The Rules Have Changed	2006	44
Mr. Blair's Explanation	2006	45
Browned Off	2006	49
On the Vietnam War Record of George Walker Bush	2006	52

Title	Year	Page
I, Putin	2006	53
Blair's Babes	2006	54
Banned Practice	2006	55
Granita Takedown	2006	56
Oh What a Lovely Jihad	2007	59
Principles	2007	61
The Sad Tale of Exeter Castle	2007	62
Miliband of the F.O.	2007	63
Please Report This to the Appropriate Authorities	2007	64
The Eternal Fight	2007	66
How Green are We	2007	67
Gordon's Stratagem	2007	68
Green	2007	69
Initiative	2007	70
Motorists Beware of Motor Cycles in Your Blind Spot	2008	71
Iraq	2008	72
Advice to the Aspiring Politician	2008	73
Warning Signs	2008	74
Questions Raised by John Prescott's Revelation …	2008	76

The Dwarf Hollyhock	2008	77
Holding Back the Tide	2008	78
In the Brown of Night	2008	78
Easy Paths	2008	79
Island	2008	80
Mantra	2008	81
Come the Man ...?	2008	82
The Redneck and the Wormhole	2008	85
The Clauses of Crime	2008	92
Lord Mandelson and the Plastic Surgeon	2008	94
Bona Headed	2007-2008	96
Bounce	2008	98
Proof	2008	99
Heroic	2008	102
Be You Never So High	2009	103
Perspective/The Rancid BLT	2009	104
Riding the Tiger	2009	110
Poor Law	2009	112
Staying Put	2009	113

Nursery Rhymes for the Modern World:

Hey-diddle-diddle	1995	115
Little Bo Peep	1995	115
Little Jack Horner	1995	115
Wee Willie Winkie	1994	116
Tony Blairy, how contrary	1998	116
The Urban Terrorist	1976	116

Foreword

This book contains all my political poetry and one or two other snippets, such as the song 'Granita Takedown' and some of the more obliquely political poems, which appear in the first section of 'Collected Poetry'. The poems have also been re-ordered so that they appear roughly in the order in which they were written. Sometimes that casts me in a rather prophetic light - 'The Tyranny of Nostalgia' anticipating the Blair that was to be by about 4 years - sometimes the reverse - 'Bona Headed' being a rebuff to an excuse used almost two years previously. With real work intervening to interrupt the completion of this volume, I have taken the introductions to the Political Poetry sections from the first and second editions of my 'Collected Poetry' and reproduced them here with some slight revisions to that from the second edition. Those wishing to avoid a hefty chunk of polemic prose should move straight on to the poetry.

RAWDON CROZIER

March 2010

Introduction to the Political Poetry Section of the Second Edition of 'Collected Poetry'

The original introduction to this book was completed when Tony Blair was still Prime Minister and John Reid, Home Secretary. The thaw between Tony Blair and Gordon Brown just happened in time for me to re-work the ending of 'Browned Off', which appeared in the first edition, and, sooner than many expected, Gordon duly succeeded Tony by a process of acclamation. For a person who professed that he wanted to have a contested election, Gordon Brown was remarkably reluctant to stop his lieutenants continuing to gather nominations after the required 40 signatures had been achieved; the result was that no-one else could find 40 members of the Parliamentary Labour Party to sign their nomination and no election took place and no-one very much seemed to mind because Gordon WASN'T TONY.

      I can't find it in myself to denigrate the simple virtue of not-being-Tony-Blair, indeed as readers who struggle through this introduction to the first will discover, I am rather proud of not-being-Tony-Blair myself, but the 'Brown bounce' caught me quite off guard. Gordon Brown was, after all, one of the original architects of "New Labour" and his significant disagreements with Tony Blair were personal rather than political, so quite why he should have been able to make so much of not-being-Tony-Blair as he did is beyond me, but he did - and particularly with the press. To read some of Gordon Brown's early notices, one would have thought that Tony Blair had been succeeded by the love-child of Cicero, Winston Churchill and God (a metaphor, the detail of which is best not thought about too closely). Of course, Gordon Brown was lucky, there were an awful lot of crises in his early premiership for which he could not be blamed and to which the appropriate response was to go around looking grave and Prime Ministerial - and looking grave has never been a particular problem for Gordon Brown. He also came up with one rather good wheeze, the 'Government of all the Talents', which briefly wrong-footed his opponents. If I had remained political and ever found myself Prime Minister, I would have had a 'Government of all the Talents', though I might actually have pushed the boat out and found *some* talent to appoint. For my part, a government which did not include Shami Chakrabarti as Home Secretary could not lay claim to being one "of *all* the talents". Having said that, I was briefly non-plussed by the appointment, in Jacqui Smith, of a Home Secretary who didn't appear to go red in the face and froth at the mouth. One of her early outings - that which followed the attempted Glasgow Airport bombing - actually seemed commendably restrained. Not all the omens were good, however: I don't know whether it is actually possible to buy a scratchcard which appoints one as Home Secretary, but her general expression - one of slightly strained bemusement - suggested, not only that such a scratchcard exists, but that Jacqui Smith had won the jackpot and been whisked away to high office, without the shopping for which she had actually just popped out, and was still trying to work out where she had left it. Once she had been in office for some time and set about promoting exactly the same sort of labyrinthine, oppressive, ill-conceived, and unintelligible legislation as all her predecessors, however, the truth became apparent - that she was different in only one respect, which was that she happened to be the most boring person on the planet. When speaking on anything of less moment than an airport bombing, she was catatonically, mind-bendingly dull. She probably was doing her equivalent of going red in the face and frothing at the mouth; it was just that for someone of her emotional range, not-sounding-as-if-you-had-just-been-lobotomised was a bit of a stretch. It is a testament to the determination of those members of Parliament who still believe in civil liberties that, by the end of the 42-day detention saga, there was anyone left awake to vote the measure down. Of course, as it was voted down in the Lords, not being in the same room may have helped but, as Jacqui Smith's dullness could penetrate nuclear bunkers, I do not stint my praise on that account.

Since I last revised this introduction, Jacqui Smith has been succeeded by another (possibly more than one) crashing non-entity, whose name (or names) in common with most of his (or her? or their) Cabinet colleagues I simply cannot be bothered to summon up the energy to recall. That's the insidious thing about living in a mediocracy (no that's not a misprint) the incessant third-ratedness dulls everything after a while, anger, intellect, satire ...

In any event, the early days of Gordon Brown's premiership were creatively quite barren for me, so it was fortunate that he subsequently contrived to be more inspirational - though I am not sure the misery and financial chaos he has played a full part in creating are not a little bit of a high price to pay for a few more poems.

The new crop of poems requires rather less in the way of explanation than the previous set, written as they have been in the space of two, rather than twenty, years. 'The Clauses of Crime' perhaps requires the most, in that its roots lie in something outside common knowledge, being inspired by an anecdote told by former civil servant, Professor Gloria Laycock, to Michael Blastland on an 'Analysis', broadcast on Radio 4 on the 6th. November 2008. Amazing as it may seem, the statistic at the start of the poem is true. The poem first appeared on the 'Analysis' website and I am grateful to Professor Laycock and 'Analysis' editor, Hugh Levinson for the their kind comments about it. The programme, "Dead Cert", highlighted the corrosive effect of the perceived need for certainty on the political process and should be compulsory listening for any aspiring politician. Of the other poems, there is one foray into American politics, 'The Redneck and the Wormhole', thematically inspired by Mark Twain's 'A Connecticut Yankee in King Arthur's Court', of which I am rather proud. Otherwise, the dreaded Blair still features to a degree and the idiocy of modern government and the emptiness and hypocrisy of modern political rhetoric is a constant theme.

If that makes me sound reactionary, the reader misunderstands me: the politics of the moment centres around an unhealthy and mutually abusive tripartite relationship between the press, the public and the political classes - we have a good line in unhealthy and mutually abusive tripartite relationships in this county - in the post-War years right up to the end of the 1970s it was that between Government, management and the unions, which almost brought the county to its knees - and the present one is, in its own way, no less damaging. First there is a general feeling that a government or opposition which does not possess an obscenely bulging portfolio of policies is not really doing its job properly. I remember this criticism being levelled in the press at John Major's government some years ago and, lo and behold, came rail privatisation. Second, there tends to be an assumption that whenever something goes wrong, or is perceived to be a problem, it just requires another piece of major legislation, or perhaps some sweeping piece of re-organization, to put everything right. Sometimes that may be so, but no thought is given to the practical consequences of sweeping change, its unintended side-effects and, what are, very often, the catastrophically high costs involved. Better, less radical, solutions get overlooked. Given the task of cracking open the proverbial nut, the average politician will look despairingly at the proffered sledgehammer and ask "Haven't you got something bigger?" It is so nice for a politician to be able to say "I am doing something" and to sound "bold" and "innovative" and to be able to say he is being "bold and innovative" (just in case we hadn't noticed that was how he was trying to sound) that the rational (and usually correct) answer that things are bound to go wrong from time-to-time and the best and most cost-effective thing we can do is to try to make the existing system work a little better is invariably not given. Harold Wilson was once accused by Willie Whitelaw of "Going round the country stirring up apathy" but, if the jibe had been directed at a Home Secretary discharging his functions at the Home Office, rather than at Wilson's electioneering style, it would have been high praise indeed. In Jacqui Smith, of course, we finally found a Home Secretary with an unprecedented capacity for stirring up apathy and it was sad to see her one obvious talent being wasted. As it is, however, press, public and Government, hype themselves into a legislative frenzy - it matters not which of them at any given time is providing the impetus, the county behaves like a dog chasing its tail, with all the wasted effort that implies, but without the benefit of deriving any enjoyment from the exercise. Another analogy might be with the drowning man who keeps flailing even when rescue is at hand and so drags the rescuer down with him, save that in this case there is no rescuer, just three drowning men each pulling the next inexorably to the bottom. I am not a reactionary, but a radical: having fewer ideas should be the next big one. Before that can happen, there needs to be a sea-change in opinion and one on a scale similar to that Margaret Thatcher wrought at the end of the 1970s. The benefits of not having another criminal justice act, another sweeping departmental reform or, please God, another computer system, need to become generally appreciated or we will remain stuck in this destructive cycle. If one returns to the analogy of the drowning man, the accepted cure for flailing is to punch him very hard in the face - insofar as that needs to be administered to any tabloid editor, journalist or politician, I volunteer, and will start work just as soon as we have a new criminal justice act to make it legal.

November 2008/April 2010

Introduction to the Political Poetry Section of the First Edition of 'Collected Poetry'

A frequent source of inspiration for my poetry has come from the practice or mis-practice of politics. On the subject of politics, I am a cynic. I believe that, for the most part, the greatest ambition a politician should have is to be a little less crap than whoever went before him. I realise that for whoever succeeds our present Prime Minister, that is setting the bar almost pitifully low; but that might actually make the goal achievable - though almost certainly not by Gordon Brown.

It may be that the reader will detect in the following poems something of an antipathy towards Tony Blair and I ought perhaps to explain the shameful reason for that antipathy, which is that I could so easily have become him.

From an early age I was fiercely political; when I grew out of dreaming about becoming an astronaut, I started to dream about becoming Prime Minister. I got involved. I helped with canvassing in local elections and that sort of thing and then a school friend of mine, Tim Skeet, who was the son of one of our local MPs, Sir Trevor Skeet, did a talk at school about what it was like to have a father who was an MP. Trevor Skeet was one of that sadly vanishing breed of decent, hard-working and independent-minded MPs, who had a life and a career beyond politics. When he did get into Parliament he developed an area of expertise (the energy industry) and applied himself to it and he made friends with fellow MPs of all persuasions – when he died in 2004 the warm and affectionate obituary which appeared in

'The Independent' was written by Tam Dayell. But during the course of my friend Tim's talk, I looked, in the sense of really looking, for the first time, at some of his election campaign material. There was, and I went away and checked what some of his opponents had produced, so I can say this with certainty, nothing strikingly original or unusual about Tim's father's campaign leaflets; they were entirely typical. They had the standard sort of blurb and, to make it more interesting and easier on the eye, the blurb was interspersed with photographs; there in the first photograph was Tim's father standing in a pose suggesting that great oratory was in progress, the effect ruined only by the fact that he was addressing a stack of bricks - brick-making was an important industry in the constituency. In the second photograph he was seen to be striking a pose of great attentiveness and concern, such as would have assured any of his prospective constituents that here was a man whose reserves of attentiveness and concern were almost without bound, and indeed the constituents in the photograph seemed themselves to have been so affected, the power of the photograph being marred only marginally by the fact that the constituents in question were actually cows - farming was quite important in the constituency too. In the third photograph, Tim's father's expression and stance were harder to make out because his head was enveloped in a silly hat - some industry that required workers to wear silly hats was also big in the constituency. I have no doubt Tim's father took all this in his stride, having had a grounding in something, less, well, stupid, to give him a clear perspective on the world but, in a moment of utter clarity and foresight, I imagined what it would be like for me to come out of school and pass straight into that sort of lifestyle. First, there would be student politics, then council elections, then parliamentary elections, each one involving their own varieties of addressing bricks, listening to cows and wearing silly hats (it was electronics, by the way – that involved wearing silly hats in Bedford). How much of me would be left? How much of my substance, of my soul, would there be by the time I actually got into a position to do anything significant? How much, if I had to do all of that on the way there? "Nothing" was the clear and unequivocal answer I gave myself. I did not know it then, of course, but what I had had was a premonition of what it would be like to be Tony Blair.

    I write this acknowledging that there is a school of thought that Blair has somehow become a more substantial figure, a Man of Purpose, since embarking on the 'War on Terror' and invading Iraq. How Orwell must be kicking himself beyond the grave for not having thought of the 'War on Terror' for '1984'; conjuring up an enemy sufficiently sinister and chilling to justify a perpetual state of emergency and yet too amorphous and ill-defined ever to be successfully defeated or appeased; every would-be tyrant's dream date, but I digress. Has Tony Blair become a man of substance? I even heard the excellent Matthew Parris, albeit in mock sympathy, saying on the radio something along the lines of "poor Tony, everyone hated him for having no beliefs, and then he went and found some, and everyone hated him more for that". I am unpersuaded; the man who once grandly introduced ill-considered and half-baked constitutional reforms as one of the most significant pieces of legislation the nation has ever known, whose thought processes about criminal justice legislation seem to begin and end with the sound-bite or the press release and who can barely pass breath without announcing some pledge, policy or initiative is of exactly the same sort as the person who goes to war with an ill-considered and half-baked plan for post-war reconstruction and so loses the peace. The thing is that while one can casually pass from one piece of bad legislation to another without too many people remembering what went before, wars are visible and don't go away; troops are on the ground, casualties are lost; so of course Blair is going to be outwardly more focussed on Iraq than, say, delivering the return of NHS dentistry. It doesn't mean he has suddenly acquired some substance.

The hypothesis fails on a second ground too, it assumes that his underlying motivation has remained constant, when patently it has not; once Blair wanted to promise the earth: reduced class sizes, creating a beacon for Western Democracy, they were all part of the mix that must have sounded good when rehearsed into the shaving mirror by an aspiring statesman anticipating the glory that was to come his way; now a tireder face looks back from the mirror, the statesman is no longer in a position to aspire, but he looks forward nonetheless to how history will write his story; now what he rehearses is looking sturdy and resolute in adversity, he will talk of tough decisions and he will still smile at himself each morning and he will never notice that the resolve he now professes is every bit as empty as were the promises he once made in the confident expectation that he had but to utter them for the job to be done and the promise fulfilled.

Believe me, I know the type; that is why I distrust and despise with the vehemence of a reformed addict these political tyros and this burgeoning political class, who know nothing apart from politics and, as a result, very little of that either.

Apart from the two valedictions at the end of this section [now at the beginning], the poems, which follow, were written during the periods of the last two governments. The casual reader might assume that they were all directed at that of Tony Blair and, were I to say that 'Anger' was written during an era of legislative idiocy piloted by a legislatively incontinent Home Secretary, who regularly indulged in pique-laden attacks on the Bar and the judiciary, students of recent history would observe how redolent of New Labour were all those traits and come to the same conclusion; but the Home Secretary in question was the last Tory Home Secretary, Michael Howard, although it has to be said his blueprint has been much-copied and refined by his "New" Labour successors. If Michael Howard was legislatively incontinent, his successors have been triply so; the Home Office under New Labour has passed, excreted and vomited criminal justice acts and probably has a nasty legislative discharge from its nose as well. Public expressions of anger and dissent at adverse court decisions and attacks on the legal system now seem a part of a Home Secretary's traditional duties. Given the relative degree of equanimity with which the great majority of unsuccessful litigants bear adverse Court decisions, one might have thought it detracted from the dignity of one of the three great offices of state to give rein to childish tantrums in such circumstances but that, apparently, is not the view of the modern Home Secretary.

Similarly 'The Tyranny of Nostalgia' was not inspired by Tony Blair but by a phrase used by his predecessor, John Major, in a speech in 1993. It is truly remarkable to see, with hindsight, just how much Tony's Blair's "New" Labour must have hated the Tories to have copied not only some of their successes (Gordon Brown's reputation for "prudence" for example is largely built on his having cribbed Ken Clarke's homework for two years) but almost all their failures; re-reading 'The Tyranny of Nostalgia', I sometimes wonder whether even the "New" in "New Labour" didn't come about as a result of recycling some Tory cast-off.

The other remarkable thing is the degree to which barristers like me were convinced that the justice system could have no worse custodians than those John Major had appointed; surely Michael Howard was about as bad as any Home Secretary could reasonably get and no Lord Chancellor could turn more against the legal profession than Lord Mackay of Clashfern? How wrong we were.

Michael Howard became remembered as comparatively benign and enlightened (long before he actually tried becoming benign and enlightened) once Jack Straw had become ensconced in his place. What had appeared stiff-necked and high-handed, while Lord Mackay was in office, seemed nothing more than a loveable prickliness, once the self-styled New Wolseley, Lord Irvine, had become installed on the Woolsack. A member of my chambers, incidentally, became a full Recorder not long after Lord Irvine had been appointed and proudly produced at some gathering his bit of parchment (or what passes for parchment these days), duly sealed and signed "Lord Irvine C."; such was the respect in which Lord Irvine was held, that there was momentarily a hushed silence, as the thought simultaneously struck each one of us that the "C." might equally well have stood for something pithier and more Anglo-Saxon than "Chancellor", and we were all reduced to helpless laughter.

Straw and Irvine, in turn, were supplanted by David Blunkett and Lord Falconer; an exponential increase in awfulness. What is more, Lord Irvine has since become mourned as the last defender of civil liberties in the Cabinet (although at time of writing, Lord Goldsmith may just have submitted an application for that long-vacant position).

When describing Charlie Falconer as "awful", I ought perhaps qualify that by saying that on a personal level, he is an extremely affable individual; it is to his twin roles as custodian of the legal system and head of the judiciary that his awfulness is confined. One has to remember that Charlie Falconer was appointed by Tony Blair as Secretary of State for Constitutional Affairs, Blair having thought in a rush of blood to the head, extreme even by his standards, that he could simply abolish the post of Lord Chancellor by dictat and without the need for any primary legislation. It is a testament to the degree to which Lord Falconer is prepared to go with the flow that he was happy to be appointed on such terms (all the more so because his ministerial title was so close to that of the fictional Jim Hacker's position as "Secretary of State for Administrative Affairs" in 'Yes Minister' - but 'New' Labour has never had much of a sense of irony or self-awareness, how else could it have seemed sensible to so many Cabinet Ministers to attempt to pass off one of the many Blair-Brown spats as "just a difference in tone"). The problem is that in Lord Falconer one has a Lord Chancellor who is essentially quiescent, more than happy to be guided by the whims of his more opinionated colleagues. An overtly hostile Lord Chancellor may be difficult to deal with (as a member of the governing body of the Western Circuit a few years ago, I saw, not at first hand but at close second hand, the problems the Bar had in dealing with one of those) but at least one is dealing with the person whose views need to be changed; hostility can be blunted by well-marshalled arguments. A quiescent Lord Chancellor is impossible, a disaster; one is no longer dealing directly with the person who is formulating policy, one is arguing with the monkey not the organ grinder, so even if the Lord Chancellor is argued round to a sensible point of view, he will then be the one having to put your case to his much more dynamic, stronger minded and more deeply entrenched Cabinet colleagues, who are driving the agenda. The result is that if the Treasury wants Charlie to delay a long-promised pay review for criminal barristers, that is just what Charlie will do, if the Home Secretary wants to further erode civil liberties, it seems he will go along with that as well.

Beyond acting as a buffer (between the Government and the legal profession, that is) it is extremely hard to figure just what is Lord Falconer's function in Government; perhaps as Tony Blair's former flatmate, he became adept at making the tea and perhaps now it is due to him that, when they meet, every member of the Cabinet has enough of their favourite type of biscuit. Who knows?

The following anecdote may give the reader some idea of his mettle. On the one occasion I met him, I taxed Lord Falconer on a rather dry but interesting piece of research done for the Legal Services Commission (Cape & Moorhead 'Costs Drivers in Criminal Defence Work') which suggested that the Criminal Legal Aid budget was running out of control because of incompetent legislation (successive Home Secretaries from Michael Howard onwards have been extremely quick to blame it on barristers' being greedy, an assertion which the research disproves). I expected him to try and sidestep the question or discredit the paper's findings but, no, he accepted them completely. So, I asked, shouldn't Parliament be given a properly costed projection of the financial implications of all new criminal justice legislation when bills are put before the House? "No" he instantly blustered "I don't think it would be a good idea at all". He paused briefly and winced, as he had done at every other mention during our meeting of anything concerning money. It seemed to me, and here, of course, I speculate, that he had conjured up a vision of his having to tell the Home Secretary, or worse, his old friend Tony that the true cost of identity cards would be three times what the government had thus far admitted and that when the computer didn't work (just try and name a publicly funded computer project that has ever come in problem-free, on-time and under-budget) and the entire population of Manchester had ended up being arrested as illegal immigrants, the resulting claims for compensation would put 3p on the rate of income tax. He recomposed himself quickly, however, and paused only a second longer before finding some overwhelming logic to counter the sense of my suggestion: "It would be like telling politicians … not to be politicians" he said and, with a note of triumph in his voice, moved on to another topic.

As for Charles Clarke, I wrote in an earlier version of this introduction (there were a good many enforced revisions over this summer) "on the question of whether it will actually prove possible … for him to be a worse Home Secretary than David Blunkett, the judgement of history is awaited". Actually judgement came rather sooner than history could manage and Charles Clarke came and went so swiftly, that it wasn't until he'd told us himself in an interview some time after his departure that anyone noticed that he had departed from tradition and hadn't had a pop at the judiciary during his short spell in office.

It is on John Reid that a verdict is now awaited. The early signs are not good. He has already shown an admirable facility for passing the buck by almost instantly on appointment branding his department "not fit for purpose". I hold no particular brief for the Home Office, nor for the Civil Service generally, but over the period during which the Labour Government has held power it has been responsible for promoting legislation which has introduced over 3,000 new criminal offences to English Law, there have also been successive legislative amendments to sentencing, criminal procedure and evidence, to say nothing of a myriad of initiatives and agendas – the majority under the auspices of the Home Office. Parliamentary draftsmen are meant to be clever people but try discerning that by reading almost any piece of modern criminal justice legislation; much of it is not simply turgid and impenetrable but actually incomprehensible - so incomprehensible that even those who have promoted it and drafted it cannot accurately say how it will work in practice. There is no need to take my word for this, this is what Lord Justice Rose, The Vice President, had to say on the subject in the case of R. v. Bradley [2005] EWCA Crim. 20:

" It is in the public interest that the criminal law and its procedures, so far as possible, be clear and straightforward so that all those directly affected, in particular, defendants, victims, the police, the probation service, jurors, lawyers for defence or prosecution, judges and magistrates, professional and lay, should be readily able to understand it. Sadly the provisions of the Criminal Justice Act 2003, which we have had to consider on this appeal, are, as is apparent, conspicuously unclear in circumstance where clarity could easily have been achieved. It is not this Court's function to identify whether the government, Parliament or Parliamentary draftsmen are responsible for this perplexing legislation. It is this Court's duty loyally to glean from the statutory language, if it can, Parliament's intention and this we have sought to do in the face of obfuscatory language. The public is entitled to know of the difficulties which such legislation creates for all concerned. The point is graphically highlighted in the present case, because the Crown have advanced to this Court a construction of the statute which is completely contrary to that suggested by the Home Office press release on the day the provisions came into force.
" It is more than a decade since the late Lord Taylor of Gosforth CJ called for a reduction in the torrent of legislation affecting criminal justice. Regrettably, that call has gone unheeded by successive governments. Indeed,

the quantity of such legislation has increased and its quality has, if anything, diminished. The 2003 Act has 339 sections and 38 schedules and runs to 453 pages. It is, in pre-metric terms, an inch thick. The provisions which we have considered have been brought into force prematurely, before appropriate training could be given by the Judicial Studies Board or otherwise to approximately 2,000 Crown Court and Supreme Court judges and 30,000 magistrates. In the meantime, the judiciary and, no doubt, the many criminal justice agencies for which this Court cannot speak, must, in the phrase familiar during the Second World War "make do and mend". That is what we have been obliged to do in the present appeal and it has been an unsatisfactory activity, wasteful of scarce resources in public money and judicial time."

Bradley was decided in January 2005 and, if we had a media interested in covering matters of substance, it should have made headlines. Were any lessons learned? No. In the run up to the 2005 General Election, the Government was so desperate not to lose pieces of legislation in the pipeline that commencement orders were issued like confetti. A clerk in Plymouth Magistrates' Court told me that he had had to start subscribing to a private on-line service to discover what law was actually in force because official notifications were not arriving in time.

One might have thought that the politicians would begin to associate Home Office failings, spiralling legal aid bills and a myriad of other problems with their own failings as legislators but as the Lord Chancellor himself has said you can't expect politicians not to behave like politicians. It may be that John Reid is right that the Home Office is unfit for purpose but one has to ask what that purpose is? And if it be to drown us all in a welter of bad legislation does one not have to go to ask whether it is not the Government itself that is truly unfit for purpose? For my part, I think that if the Government were it able to drag itself up to the level of passable mediocrity that is the most one can reasonably expect from a government, the Home Office could probably do the same.

This section ought to include some acknowledgements, and, those who read 'On Journalism', may be surprised to see that those I wish to thank are all journalists. I only know them through their columns, but the research necessary to write something like 'Obituary' would have been, if not impossible, certainly very much harder (and well beyond my thin reserves of patience), without their unwitting assistance. They are, in no particular order, Matthew Parris of 'The Times', who for me is a sort of touchstone against which I judge my opinions, just as, in his own way, is Tony Blair. The difference is that, while there are many things upon which Tony Blair and I may well share similar views, I would always question the validity of any opinion that I knew I held in common with him. Matthew Parris and I may well hold different opinions on a whole range of subjects but, when I read one of his articles expressing an opinion with which I disagree, I always find myself questioning whether he might not be right, and, even if I conclude I have been right all along, the exercise is always worthwhile.

Nick Cohen of 'The Observer' is one of those journalists who, although left-wing, is too intelligent to be doctrinaire. He has been particularly good on "New" Labour's "dirty streak" and had he written nothing but "Darkening of a Nation" ('Observer', 26th. October 2003) he would warrant a mention but he has been invaluable on a whole range of other topics. Alan Watkins of 'The Independent on Sunday' unfailingly provides an interesting degree of perspective to events and when, as he often does, Tony Blair attempts to rewrite history, Alan Watkins can be relied upon to set the record straight. He gives the impression of having been around forever and having forgotten nothing. Simon Carr of 'The Independent' has a finely tuned ear for political bull; I treasure his discovery that Hazel Blears is not only the name of a New Labour politician but also a description of what she does. Henry Porter, who now writes in 'The Observer' (and I feel very guilty about his having been so totally below my radar before that), writes wonderfully about the threat New Labour poses to our civil liberties. He is not one of those who makes the mistake of being a slightly apologetic defender of fundamental freedoms and cedes the initiative to those who have contrived to believe it is statesmanlike, brave and resolute to limit them, not realising that they are giving away our most powerful weapon. It is our concept of personal freedom that dictators and theocrats really fear; dilute it too much and we are no longer fighting for freedom and democracy but engaging in a murky squabble between competing shades of tyranny.

2006

On the Resignation of Harold Wilson

And so he quietly slipped from public view,

And but a scandal marked the spot where one the titles grew.

1978

Lines on the Resignation of Cecil Parkinson

So farewell Cecil Parkinson,

Who tried so hard to please.

Still wearing bonds of marriage

Because you threw away the Keays.

What you did was not so bad,

You just ran out of luck,

Because as Perry Worthsthorne might have said

"No-one really gave a fuck"

1985

On Journalism

It is said of all Professions, Whoring and Politics came first

And that from their sordid union, Gossip next did burst,

She was no Profession but once was known by Blame

And from that second sordid union Journalism came.

Raised on alcohol and envy and tutored in deceit,

The brutish infant monster quickly found its feet.

In seedy Fleet Street lairs it multiplied and its progeny were sent

To seek out scandal where they could, and where they failed, to invent.

Since small in mind and vile, they were, they assumed a fair disguise

As guardians of morality and enemies of lies,

An Honourable Profession, committed to conform,

Their actions guided solely by their duty to inform.

And if it is true, that there are some worthy of this claim,

They only serve to better camouflage a thousand others' shame,

Who pander to man's darker side, the voyeuristic lust,

For enjoying sin is moral, if mingled with disgust.

When a man commits adultery, true censure's quickly said,

Without any need for detail of what was done in bed.

But the journalist, in censure, is as often writing porn,

Concealing titillation with simulated scorn.

If the Gods first visit madness on those they would destroy,

Journalism's children a viler sport enjoy,

They visit on their victims, not madness first, but fame,

For the better-known the victim, the easier the claim,

That it is for the public good the story has been told,

The better hid the motive that papers must be sold.

And if the story's spiced a little too, it is for the public good they act,

Readers must be entertained, not left with dull and boring fact.

But do not forget, two perpetuate these lies,

The Journalist who writes them, and the Fool who buys.

The sneering and the envy sap the Nation's will

And even if we know it, we are yet corrupted still.

And day by day the cancer grows a little more with every proof,

Lies cloaked in feigned morality behind a mask of Truth.

And all the while from every gutter the carrion glibly cry:

"The Press defends your freedom, so it cannot lie,

though it may sometimes give the innocent a little to deny".

1979-91

Anger

Of all my Muses,

Most prolific and most real

Is the anger

That I often feel

But as I watch

This Nation's spirit die,

My mind goes blank,

My pen runs dry.

                                            1992

The Tyranny of Nostalgia

Cast down the tyranny of the old,

The nostalgia for a gentler life,

Reform the formed, recast the mould,

And prosper through the ceaseless strife.

Forget tradition and reflection,

Reason too be cast aside,

Change shall be our one direction,

Constancy no more our guide.

Change the laws, change education,

Better, change them annually,

Change shall be our one salvation

Let Britain never settled be.

      1993

Questions

What is it makes an incisive mind,

When turned inwards,

Small and blind?

Why it is great intelligence,

Or power, or wealth

So often make a man

Incompetent to judge himself?

And how can we ever hope

To make a rational selection

Of our leaders

When we know

Talent will vanish on election?

                                              1993

On a Tree Dying in the Strand

As a sapling young you struggled hard,

O'ercast by shadows of baronial walls

And by the shade of vain, capricious monarchs' power

Until at last there came the day

When trunk now broad and branches high

You cast a shadow over them

That once held power unchecked.

But later gardeners, careless of their charge,

Now prune the branch and trim the bough,

That cast protective shade,

And to the elements and crueller shadows now expose

The poor, the weak and derelict.

                                            2003

Obituary

This poem's written more in hope than expectation,

Of an event to cheer the Nation,

But imagine now and in your mind's eye shout "Hooray"

We bury Tony Blair today.

Let not tradition, reticence, no, nor drab convention,

Guide us now in what we choose or fail to mention.

He had no regard for them and in his "New" world nor must we

But with a clear, untrammelled eye let us now assess the man he
      used to be.

He had a certain charm, this we must allow, if only to excuse,

Those trusting souls who voted for the charm

And forgot to enquire about his views.

Yet the charm was superficial, a mere confected skin,

Like chocolate round an Easter egg, which conceals a void within.

But of his views,

If he had been asked, just what would he have said?

"What do you believe?" was the only question in the House that
      ever stopped him dead.

But do not call him faithless, for of Faith he had an ample store;

He believed what he believed without ever needing more

Than his private inner truth, which endured, undaunted and

      intact,

Even in the face of reason or any contrary fact.

From his tale of youthful derring-do as a teenage stowaway

To his many grand pronouncements on the issues of the day.

With what self-righteous passion he gilded each deceit

When his blast against conservatism brought the Labour

      conference to its feet.

Did he know or did he not care about the hist'ry he re-wrote;

Claiming Beveridge and Keynes (who were Liberals)

And that a Labour Government gave women the vote.

On Question Time (on TV) he announced a hunting ban

With faux-blokeish sincerity and cynical élan.

"Why I voted against hunting" he said and paused, not for

      conscience, but effect.

Did he not recall he hadn't done, that what he said was incorrect?

Or could it be that when he spoke it, he somehow made it true?

And that by that standard there was proof of Iraqi weapons too?

The Chief of the Defence Staff never was misled;

The case for war was clear and unequivocal, at least, inside
     Blair's head.

And then there were his promises, which in the future would be
     met;

Did he ever think they would be, or did he trust that people
     would forget

Just what it was he'd promised, when the promises fell due

Or would simply be distracted when he promised something new?

No infant classes over thirty by 09.02

Was one promise not delivered; there were countless others too.

"Health Service dentistry for all" still hasn't happened yet

Though in '99 Blair promised it "within 2 years" through NHS
     Direct.

But he was no habitual liar and, should you need the proof,

Lord Hutton listened to him and heard him speak only the truth.

In fact most often when he spoke, Blair said nothing very much,

If you discounted all the flannel, big promises and such.

On almost any issue, "X", he would address the matter so:

"We will seize the opportunity of change, I want you all to know,

we will approach X with integrity, respect and dedication

to empower our new more-just society with can-do innovation

there is a brand-new ethos, a fundamental shift,

and as we strive for excellence, we will not let X drift.

We will push for ever-higher standards in the challenges we
        meet,

with effective leadership..." (The well-drilled audience will have
        risen to its feet)

And with a final flourish what an ovation he collects

With "Our number one priority is X, X, X, X, X".

It should be no surprise that when elected, he chose to champion
        the Dome

In its vast and soulless structure the empty politician must have
        felt at home.

And from an empty public building he progressed to empty
        constitutional reform,

Introduced with all the empty passion which ever was his norm.

It was "New" and "Innovative", let nobody be in doubt,

Not least the decision to announce it before he'd worked any
      details out.
But planning was an element he often seemed to lack;
What exactly was the plan for building "New" Iraq?
How many terrorists were recruited while law and order
      crumbled?
How many died once the war was won, because winning peace
      was fumbled?
There is so much more to cover, so very little time,
The funeral procession is progressing and first there comes a line
Of past and present Spin-Doctors lead by Campbell and, further
      back, Jo Moore
And then Special Advisers follow, score, by score, by score.
Then come Labour benefactors, each bearing a wreath,
"From a tobacco advertising ban" says Ecclestone's "your
      Government gave F1 relief
and your party gave my million back, which was good beyond
      belief"

Mittal's just says: "Man of Steel", Desmond's: "Condolences

        Expressed",

Enron's: "Your Government had energy, you were a great success"

"You and Mr. Brown" says Andersen's "ended our public sector

        purdah

and one day, we hope he'll take our relationship still further"

Now come Blair's faithful Ministers, the present and the past,

Advancing at respectful pace, 'til the grave is reached at last.

The Ministers form an Honour Guard and what an array

Of all their varied qualities they brazenly display;

The rubbish, briefly infamous, the vacuous, piss-poor:

Mandelson, Robinson, Harman, Byers, Blunkett, Straw,

Kelly, Clarke and Hewitt and Lord Irvine too

Brown and Prescott stand ahead, last obeisance to do.

Lord Falconer (the Minister for Voids) has prepared the grave

Into which Blair's coffin, now, respectfully is laid

And with it, like a Pharaoh's with trophies surrounded,

Caskets of ancient, hard-earned, liberties are dutif'ly impounded.

The Spin-Doctors, in chorus, sing Blair's praises all around,

While other news, they wish to hide, is whispered to the ground.

And upon the tomb by way of epitaph, the following I'd set:

"He was no despot nor dictator, but should his passing cause
      regret,

Remember,

The public trust he squandered was not his to cast aside,

All Government becomes suspect once that trust has died,

That he acted from expedience, not from evil, does not mitigate
      the wrong,

The way he lied, yet was elected, left Democracy less strong."

2004-2005

The Spin-Doctor's Daughter

The Spin-Doctor saw his little daughter

Trip and fall into the water.

The bank was steep, she couldn't swim,

Her end was looking near and grim.

He sat himself upon the brink

As the little girl began to sink

And now he judged the time propitious

(While she was playing with the fishes)

To tell her things she ought to know

(Her little head sank very low):

"The dog is dead, the cat is ill,

Your hamster's lying strangely still";

He paused and checked with condescension

Not-drowning still held her attention

And thought the chance was Heaven-sent

To save them both embarrassment

So, with her locked in watery strife,

He expounded on the facts of life

And even, without circumspection,

On boys and sex and contraception,

Until,

With flailing limbs, and luck, and more,

His daughter spluttered to the shore.

The Spin Doctor now, his talk complete,

The bedraggled girl helped to her feet.

Well pleased, though less at her salvation,

Than with his well-timed gift of information

But, sensing her in need of cheer,

He addressed her thus, he said "My dear,

it will be fun, you'll find this week

the pets are playing hide and seek

and Dog and Hamster are so clever,

they may stay hid away for ever".

"My dear" he said "though I know not when,

One day we'll talk like this again".

2005

The Politics of Fear

There are burglars, there are paedophiles, there are drunken,

       violent yobs

Terror bombers from far-off lands, who worship different gods.

Don't take a risk,

Just think of it,

One could be your neighbour;

You can fix these people in a trice,

If only you vote Labour.

Don't risk another party now,

Some of them eat babies

And they'll put your mortgage up

And they'll give you rabies.

Labour's always honourable.

You can trust in its direction.

It won't break a single promise now, 'til after the election.

                                                           2005

The Rules Have Changed

A terrorist may need a bomb,
Or a gun,
To kill someone
But countries die in other ways
The fearful glance,
The mistrustful gaze,
Between friend and friend,
or those who should be,
bring the end
First to comfort,
Then to truth,
Then to just laws,
The need for proof.
There is no need for bomb or gun
To kill a country, just someone
in charge to lose his head
and give in to the sense of dread.

We speak so much in code today,
We lose the sense of what we say.
"The rules have changed"
Requires translation which, when done,
Means "The terrorists have won".

                                                     2006

Mr. Blair's Explanation

(for not holding an Iraq inquiry)

The message we'd send would be utterly wrong,

For the sake of the Army we have to be strong,

More important than knowing just what we got wrong.

There can be no Inquiry, of that there's no doubt -

Can you imagine just what we'd find out?

The message we'd send would be utterly wrong,

For the sake of the Army we have to be strong,

More important than knowing just what we got wrong.

There can be no Inquiry, of that there's no doubt -

Can you imagine just what we'd find out?

The Army's meant to run lean, undermanned and misled

What could an Inquiry tell us instead?

The message we'd send would be utterly wrong,

For the sake of the Army we have to be strong,

More important than knowing just what we got wrong.

There can be no Inquiry, of that there's no doubt -

Can you imagine just what we'd find out?

The Army's meant to run lean, undermanned and misled,

What could an Inquiry tell us instead?

And think of the soldiers, who'd have missed all the fight

If we'd lessened the conflict by planning it right?

The message we'd send would be utterly wrong,

For the sake of the Army we have to be strong,

More important than knowing just what we got wrong.

There can be no Inquiry, of that there's no doubt,

Can you imagine just what we'd find out?

The Army's meant to run lean, undermanned and misled,

What could an Inquiry tell us instead?

And think of the soldiers, who'd have missed all the fight,

If we'd lessened the conflict by planning it right.

The soldiers all love us, you cannot discount

The pain they would suffer,

Were we politicians brought to account.

The message we'd send would be utterly wrong,

For the sake of the Army we have to be strong,

More important than knowing just what we got wrong.

There can be no Inquiry, of that there's no doubt,

Can you imagine just what we'd find out?

The Army's meant to run lean, undermanned and misled,

What could an Inquiry tell us instead?

And think of the soldiers, who'd have missed all the fight,

If we'd lessened the conflict by planning it right?

The soldiers all love us, you cannot discount

The pain they would suffer,

Were we politicians brought to account.

And you can only imagine the pain of the men,

Should we not be there to drop them in it again.

The message we'd send would be utterly wrong,

For the sake of the Army we have to be strong,

More important than knowing just what we got wrong.

There can be no Inquiry, of that there's no doubt,

Can you imagine just what we'd find out?

The Army's meant to run lean, undermanned and misled,

What could an Inquiry tell us instead?

And think of the soldiers, who'd have missed all the fight,

If we'd lessened the conflict by planning it right?

The soldiers all love us, you cannot discount

The pain they would suffer,

Were we politicians brought to account.

And you can only imagine the pain of the men,

Should we not be there to drop them in it again.

The British soldier is loyal, how sad he would be,

If we had an Inquiry – and it blamed me!

Or suggested we ought to plan better next time –

The effect on morale! It would be such a crime!

So it's not for ourselves that we're dodging the flak,

It's for the sake of our soldiers – out in Iraq.

>   2006

Browned Off

There's a difference in Tone,

I'm not quite sure yet exactly what it is

But there's something sneaky in that smile of his

When we're alone

There's a difference in Tone.

There's a difference in Tone

He suggested and I agreed

He'd go first and then I'd lead

And he couldn't disown

Our agreement, could Tone?

There's a difference in Tone

I somehow thought he'd be gone by now

But he's still there and I'm wondering how,

Now his cover is blown,

I ever trusted him - Tone.

"There's a difference in tone"

All the Cabinet said it on the news today

"There's no disagreement" I heard them say

They let it be known

"There's just a difference in tone"

A difference in TONE!?!

I should say!

We made a deal and he threw it away!

And they say I'm unbalanced,

How could I not be?

You'd be unbalanced if you were treated like me!

Once we were friends,

Now I want to burn down his home!

(Or perhaps I should say,

I would if I didn't want to live there one day.)

He got what he wanted

And his ego has grown,

He's like a dog in a manger

With his favourite bone,

And that, if you ask me,

Is the difference in Tone.

But wait..

There's a difference in Tone,

It suddenly seems that we're friends again,

I'm not "psychologically flawed" but "the next PM",

So perhaps I'll get into Number Ten

And there won't be another moment when

I'm totally thrown

By a difference in Tone

2006

On the Vietnam War Record of George Walker Bush

How sad it is:

Folk forget and memories fade

Of the sacrifices that you made

When, for three plus years (or was it less?),

Clothed in National Guardsman's battledress,

You nobly went to serve your Nation

And keep the Homeland from invasion,

And in so doing did you eschew

The glory that must have been your due,

And gave those less lucky-born than you

The chance to spill abroad their blood less blue.

            2006

I, Putin

I'm worlds away from Yeltsin and his lawless latter days,

And were there any justice that should surely earn me praise.

I don't roll around the country like some lumb'ring drunken ox,

I'm quiet and grey and sober in my life and suit and socks.

Where what threatened was disorder and chaos and alarm,

I've re-imposed the order and a (slightly eerie) calm,

Yet former friends and critics will keep trying to expose me;

Why are so many people just dying to oppose me?

2006

Blair's Babes

This pair of Blair's best babes

Travel through their lives

Wearing rictus smiles

Of new-formed Stepford wives.

Smartly dressed outside

With completely hollow centres,

They suck out any trace of hope

Like a pair of prim Dementors

Reason flees the room

When either one appears:

Harriet befuddles,

Hazel blears.

                        2006

Banned Practice

The hunting field's a tricky place

With many perils to be faced

Among the qualities,

He who hunts requires

Are jumping over fences

And avoiding mires

To all this natural complication

Is there a need to add

Stupid, madcap legislation?

                        2006

Granita Takedown

A little pasta, a little pesto sauce,

We need a leader to save the Party

You'll run of course?

It won't be easy

But I know how hard you'll try

To rise above the jibes about

Your dourness and your glassy eye.

It won't be easy

You'll need great reserves of charm

To woo the Party

And your rivals to disarm.

It won't be easy.

That Bolognese, it looks delicious,

If a little red for me.

This could be our only chance

To seize our Destiny.

It won't be easy

You'll need lots of flair

Don't look so worried

I'm on your side, I'll help you there.

It isn't easy,

I've ambitions too

But you and I, to split the vote,

That wouldn't do.

It isn't easy.

To drink, Chianti? Or are you on beer?

I can see it on your face,

That hidden fear.

It isn't easy,

But however hard you try,

You still suspect it

That I'm the better guy.

It can't be easy

Acting for the common good

But now you see it,

As I always knew you would.

It can't be easy.

It won't be easy to lead the Party

It won't be easy to lead the Party,

It can't be easy to fear your fate,

But I can do it, lead the Party,

And if you really want to,

I can give it to you,

I can let you do it,

At some future date.

                      2006

Oh What A Lovely Jihad!

Prologue

Those Mullahs who preach Jihad,
However great they see their mission,
Never seem to wish for Martyrdom
As a personal ambition;
But if the lot of Martyrs
Really were that nice,
Would they not have blown themselves up
And sent themselves to Paradise?
Their patter somehow reminds me
Of the mulish generals of old
Who promised glory in the trenches
And squandered lives untold.

Sermon

You go on and make your sacrifice,
I'll just wait here and preach,
You have your fate and I have mine,
God needs some of us to teach.
You must understand that it's my life
I'd much sooner be giving;
It's just a burden sent by God
That I must keep on living.
So strap your bomb-belt tight, lad,
And blow yourself beyond the aid of surgeons
And you'll find yourself in Paradise

To be tended to by virgins
And trust me as your Mullah, lad,
To read aright the texts:
They'll be special Divine virgins,
Who are really good at sex -
And these promises are solid,
All proved by Divination,
As a Mullah would I indulge
In crude manipulation?
While other creeds may preach
God's Will is subtle and refined,
I can offer fantasies
Of the masturbatory kind.
So now you can see the sacrifice
I'm making for myself,
While, you will go to Paradise
With boundless sex and wealth,
I just have to go on living - well,
I suppose I'll have my health.

      2007

Principles

Torture's all right if someone else does it,

I know it's all right and can say it because it

must be morally right and ethically clean

Whatever gets done, provided nothing is seen.

And when embarking on torture or that sort of mission

You need a name for it, which invites no contrition,

And that's why we call it "External Rendition"

And that's why this whole thing's been such a lark

We've done it for ages and kept the world in the dark

And we haven't tortured, the whole point of the scheme

Is that the torturing's done by some wholly disownable brutal

                                                    regime

There's no handling scapels, nor electrodes, required,

 So nothing sullies our principles, which are rightly admired.

                                                          2007

The Sad Tale of Exeter Castle
OR Prudence in Practice

It would have cost about four million

To have put the old court right

But they didn't have the money,

Because the budget was so tight -

The budget for repairs

That is what I really meant

Because the budget for new buildings

Hadn't all been spent.

"But the old courts are decaying"

Someone said "Whatever can we do?"

And someone must have answered

"We can just build something new.

We won't need to find four million then

It will just cost twenty-two".

                        2007

Miliband of the F.O.
OR Adopt & Survive

I may be Foreign Secretary

But I've other things to do,

So if I miss some public functions

Then what is it to you?

It was just some Royal State Visit -

There'll always be another one -

Besides, I was in the USA,

Adopting my new son.

And it wasn't that important;

It was just the Saudi King

And being seen with despot's

Really not my thing

And so my brand new baby

Has helped me

Stay on moral higher ground

Though I'll need to get a bigger house

When another tyrant's visit comes around.

2007

Please Report This To the Appropriate Authorities

I'd like to chop up Tony Blair

Or electrocute him in a chair

Or push him from a rocky ledge

Or drag him backwards through a hedge

And if the latter failed to leave him dead

I later could remove his head.

Such bloody thoughts, which are inclined

To pop into the gentlest mind

And, now I come to write them down,

Must as often feature Gordon Brown

Once thus expressed are not just thoughts

But crimes to trouble solemn courts.

What a witless, scared and shrivelled Age

To make a crime of simple rage!

And how our moral force is spent

To resort to law not argument!

This is not hyperbole but fact

Under the Terrorism Act[1]

They put Samina Malik in a cell

Because what she thought

She wrote as well.

What if her views were quite abhorrent?

Or that she spouted hatred in a torrent?

I would sooner see her free

And there to be no crime in poetry.

Which brings me back to Gordon Brown;

Couldn't someone gun him down?

Or maybe, acting on a whim,

Possibly set fire to him?

[1] This poem was written between the conviction on the 8th. November 2007 of Samina Malik of an offence of possessing information of a kind likely to be useful to a person committing or preparing an act of terrorism, contrary to section 58 of the Terrorism 2000, and her subsequent sentence on the 6th. December 2007. The "information" in question included a number of poems written under the nom de plume "the Lyrical Terrorist". The Court of Appeal was subsequently able, in another case under the same section, to apply an interpretative gloss to the section and cut down the lethally wide interpretation the Crown had persuaded the judge to put on it in Samina Malik's case. Following that decision Samina Malik's own appeal against conviction was allowed in 2008.

The Eternal Fight

Though Good and Evil sometimes fight
As serried armies ranged in might
Their battles are more often fought
In the minds of men between thought and thought
And Evil's strength most often lies
Not in its strength but in its guise:
The fear for life, concern for health
The threats perceived to home and wealth
That human drive: self-preservation
Can all be turned to lead us to damnation
When deployed on Evil's side
They make us lose our moral guide
So that in our fear and in our fright
We lose the sense of what is right.
It should be clearly understood
One cannot torture and be good
Some things are an abomination
However great the provocation;
Evil needs no force of arms to win
It is enough to mire both sides in sin.

                                          2007

How Green Are We?

If the Government really cared that much

About the environment and such

They'd see where people worked and shopped

And where the trains and 'buses stopped

And consider the necessity

Of how to get from A to B

And when those things had all been heeded

They'd have houses built where they were needed

Instead, they decree that homes must drop

Far away from school and shop

Bereft of proper infrastructure

So that the transport system starts to rupture,

And when people drive, as they must do,

The Government says: "How green are you?"

To which the reply should always be

"Not so green that you can put the blame on me."

                                                          2007

Gordon's Stratagem

Me and my friend Tony, we're quite different propositions

So you simply cannot blame me for his government's decisions

I was a loyal and faithful minister, who served him at his need

So don't imagine something sinister like the thought that we
                                                                    agreed

On any point of policy for which he's taking flak

From presenting dodgy dossiers and invading Iraq

To the creeping loss of freedom and division of the Nation

And the misconceived tinkering that was triple Education.

I was just a humble Chancellor, was I given to dissent?

What could I do but follow whichever way he went?

I'm not at all like Tony; I'm a very different man

Whereas he could spin for England, I never ever span.

At least never so transparently, some still think I'm Old Labour

And they're waiting ever more impatiently 'til I supplant my
                                                                     neighbour

They think I possess a moral compass, that I'm canny and
                                                                     robust,

They're so keen to see the back of Blair, they don't peer
                                                                    beneath my crust

Just remember me as prudent, let me bulldoze through the
                                                                      facts

That I've really wasted billions and you've never paid more tax.
                                                                            2007

Green

If green taxes worked we'd be all right
A change would happen overnight
There'd never be another flight
Pumping out that CO_2;
Green tax would change the things we do.

If green taxes worked we'd shout "Hooray"
We'd walk or bike to work each day
And none of us would ever say:
"I think I'll take the car today";
Green tax would keep those jams at bay.

If green taxes worked, now here's the thing,
If they stopped our flights and motoring,
They wouldn't raise a single thing.
If green taxes worked: just face the facts
There'd have to be some other tax
For what green taxes really do,
Which is to raise more revenue.

2007

Initiative

We don't want a justice system

Just something which appears

To tick the necessary boxes

To allay the public's fears

Announcing new initiatives

Is what we do the best.

Done with enough rapidity,

It saves the awkward need

To put any to the test

And it makes us feel that we are busy

And concerned with cutting crime

And the voters get to see us

On telly all the time.

                      2007

Motorists Beware of Motorcyles in Your Blind Spot

If, for a motorcyclist,

A blind spot's such a bad place to be

And I'm in my car,

What on earth is the point in warning me?

For, if into my blind spot, he's likely to whiz,

Shouldn't someone warn him

Where my blind spot is?

                              2008

Iraq

Wars are often forced upon a nation
With the time for due consideration
Of individual pro and con
Never there, or too soon gone.
The choices are reduced to one:
Capitulate or struggle on.

Iraq was never such a war;
There was time to plan, then plan some more
And when the object was a state's salvation
There was time to plan regeneration;
We had resources and the time,
To not have used them was a crime.

When troops were marshalled on the border
There should have been, to follow, in close order,
Doctors, engineers, police,
To heal, rebuild and keep the peace,
Because when a war is won,
Few things are sooner past
Than the chance to build a peace to last.

2008

Advice to the Aspiring Politician

"Vision", "Vision", "Change" and "Change"

"New", "New", New", "New", "New"

Are words that voters like to hear

So whatever else you do

Say them lots and lots -

Oh, and did I mention "Vision"?

They never seem to lose their gloss

Nor attract derision

Say: "Vision", "New" and "Change" a lot;

It will leave no voter unaffected

They'll put a cross by your name at the Ballot Box

And you will be elected.

        2008

Warning Signs

There must be in every public building,

Displayed on window, wall and door,

Signs telling people not to smoke

For that is now the law.

And is it just that smoking

Has been singled from the crowd

Or is that without a sign

All else is now allowed.

If they didn't want a murder, say,

There ought to be a sign that said:

"Violence is prohibited,

when it results in making people dead"

And is arson now OK,

If one stick to smokeless fuels?

And robbery with menaces?

And even fighting duels?

And can we drive upon the pavement,

If we stick to legal speed?

And can we burgle people's houses,

Should we ever feel the need?

Perhaps the Government isn't stealing liberty

But giving us all more

By creating 3,000 new offences which,

Without a sign,

We'll have the freedom to ignore.

                                              2008

Questions Raised by John Prescott's Revelation that he Suffered from Bulimia in the Order They Occurred to Me

First ...

In the light of his size and his biographic admission

That when things got tough,

He'd first gobble down and then vomit up stuff

Did John Prescott remember the latter quite often enough?

Second ...

With a decade or more at the heart of the State

With every chance to commune with the Good and the Great -

His Memoirs are trailed by the way that he ate!?!

Third and last ...

When his book's been read and taken in,

Might he suddenly seem rather thin?

2008

The Dwarf Hollyhock

Any plant, a dwarf hollyhock say,

May have the chance to have its day,

And, if nearby there's no larger flower,

It may positively seem to tower;

It's just the setting makes it tall,

Objectively, of course, it's small.

I saw such a bed the other day;

A dwarf hollyhock was holding sway

Over all the other plants around,

Which grew stubbornly along the ground.

 Its planter, a disappointed horticulturist,

Had given it a satiric twist:

" I call it my New Labour bed"

In a rather rueful way he said

"and as for the hollyhock that's there,

of course, I've named it Tony Blair".

                                                2008

Holding Back the Tide

"No more boom and bust"

No-one ever has achieved it

Gordon Brown said he had;

Perhaps he actually believed it.

      2008

In the Brown of Night

They say you have a moral compass

They may even be right

But to be guided by a compass

There needs to be a source of light

And the moral fire inside you

Doesn't seem to burn that bright.

      2008

Easy Paths

When the loss of faith in conscience
And the power of remorse
Means hard punishment's demanded,
Almost as of course,
And when no distinction's made
Between the Wicked and Misguided
And the need for rehabilitation
Is forgotten or derided,
When harshness or brutality
Is re-cast as strength of mind
When Society in general
Becomes uncaring and unkind,
Then the easy paths lead downwards,
Towards chaos or repression
But it's a mistake to think the latter
Is any more desirable progression
And we can only hope our leaders
Do not shirk their load
And have the strength and courage
To seek the harder road.

2008

Island

"No man is an island"

Undeniably that's true

And in the World Economy

No island is one too.

Did Gordon Brown not know that

When he said

"No more boom and bust"?

And, if he did, why say it

And so abuse our trust?

Had he fixed

The US mortgage market?

The worldwide thirst for oil?

Or the myriad global factors

That can make inflation boil

Into something in the nature

Of *(deep breath, pause)* exp-O-nential progression?

Or those other global factors

Which can usher in recession?

At least now he's Prime Minister

He can blame that other chap,

Who called himself "Iron Chancellor",

And just say he was crap.

                              2008

Mantra

"What real people are asking..."

Is something I frequently say

"What real people are asking..."

As often as ten times a day

If a journalist asks me a question

With an answer I'm reluctant to give

"What real people are asking..."

Is the mantra by which

We political classes all live.

And it's really quite funny,

We make up the next bit as we go

Because what real people really are asking

Is something we really don't know

And on a point of translation

When we say it,

Whether it's me, or the great Mr. Blair,

It means:

"Go fish for your answer. Fuck off. I really don't care"

2008

Come the Man...?

"I have this brand new driver"

I was told lately by a friend

"And the brilliant thing about him is

There's almost nothing he can't mend.

I feel so safe, when he is driving,

It's really very nice

To know, whatever may befall me,

He can fix it in a trice

For example, he was driving me,

Just the other day,

And we ran out of petrol

And he fixed it right away

He said he didn't see it coming,

Fuel gauges being what they are,

But when it comes to finding petrol,

He's really quite a star.

And there was that other time

He drove into the wall,

He said he hadn't seen it coming

He hadn't seen it there at all.

He's exceptional at first aid,

Wound dressing, fitting slings;

It's so good to have a driver

Who knows about those things.

I don't blame him for the crash itself,

I don't blame him at all;

It's really very hard to spot

A ten-foot high brick wall

And besides,

I found myself reflecting

As I lay bleeding on the ground,

How much worse it might have been

If he hadn't been around."

I met my friend again

The other day, in town,

And he said to me "You know,

This PM, Gordon Brown?"

"I'm very glad we've got him

It's really very nice

To think however bad the crisis

He will fix it in a trice.

He reminds me of my driver

As much as anybody can

I suppose it's just good fortune,

Come the moment, come the man."

                                  2008

The Redneck and the Wormhole

The Redneck lived, as rednecks will,

In a trailer park beside a hill,

He drove his pickup every day

To the five-and-dime to earn his pay

And each day he could, he drank his fill

Of beer, or something from a still.

He knew nothing of an inner life.

In times of stress he beat his wife

Or if he really needed fun

He'd drive somewhere and shoot his gun

At anything he could attack

Whether rabbit, buck or Black

Perhaps a Jew if one passed by

'Most anything that caught his eye –

Don't brand this as discrimination

He hated almost every nation

And almost every race and creed

And folk with whom he disagreed.

In fact, his ornery-ness was such

He didn't even like most rednecks much

But of all the things his temper fired

Liberals, by far, most hate inspired

And, in short order, next he hated

The wealthy and the educated

Except George Walker Bush, of blesséd name

Who could not help his family's shame,

Their money and their education,

But with a redneck's heart still ruled the Nation.

For the Redneck had a softer side

One thing could make him swell with pride

And sometimes even make him cry

Independence Day – the Fourth July,

When, surely rednecks, such as he,

Had thrown off British tyranny.

The beer, the Flag, the Flag, the beer

Made those old events seem very near

And so he'd shed his manly tear

And then he'd go and drink more beer…

And then more beer and them some more

Until, collapsing to the floor,

"God bless America" he'd say

And then, unconscious, sleep a day.

_____

One Fourth July, the day he'd spent

In this drunken sacrament

And, waking in his local bar,

He'd set off home, which wasn't far,

But the beer had taken such a toll

He never made his trailer goal,

Instead he stumbled down a hole.

For his very life, he feared:

"A well" he thought, and disappeared.

_____

Now Fate decreed the Redneck fell

Not down some ordinary well

But through a wormhole back in time

He travelled by its twisted line

To emerge, as it were, in mid-oration

At the founding moment of his Nation.

Some time around July the First

As the Declaration was rehearsed

By Jefferson, every inch the country gent,

Educated and intelligent,

His speech inspired by Liberal Zeal –

And how, you ask, did the Redneck feel?

Did tears of joy well up inside?

Did his redneck heart just swell with pride?

_____

Well no.

Time travel can stimulate the brain

But leaves base intellect the same,

So, synapses firing in all directions,

The Redneck started making strange connections

It was as if he'd never heard

The Indictment against George the Third,

For some things the Indictment said were crimes

Seemed redolent of modern times

And his President with kingly name,

Whose actions seemed ... somehow ... the same!

"Refused ... laws ... most wholesome for the common good"

G.W. vetoed infant healthcare - as he should!

The torture ban he'd vetoed too -

And that was right, in the Redneck's view -

"... depriving ..." the Redneck's hackles rose in fury

"... the benefit of trial by jury."

Did they not think, did they not know

Ol' Bush would do that at Guantanamo?

"...transporting..." and "...beyond the seas..."

Lodged in his mind but did not please

The Redneck, with its parallel

With rendition flights to - who could tell?

And so these bold denunciations

Of King George's depredations

Left the Redneck quite aghast

At the rebuke to his present by the past.

And the debate progressed around the floor,

'Til the Redneck could hold back no more:

"You Goddammed Pinko Liberal Scum"

He yelled and, speaking thus, pulled out his gun

And promptly slaughtered everyone.

_____

And thus the Redneck, by his crime,

Changed the later course of time.

Of course, he reaped his just rewards:

Elevated to the House of Lords.

Of Jefferson's views, no-one now talks;

They build guys of him, just like Guy Fawkes.

And Lord Redneck, he still got to cry

Each Summer Bonfire Night, the First July

_____

From this sad tale there was some bounty;

Each State became an English county

And George Walker Bush wears yellow spats

Instead of favouring cowboy hats

And everyone forgives this sin

Because no-one's ever heard of him.

2008

The Clauses of Crime

Four per cent of all victims

Account for more than forty per cent of all crime

Which means that a small group of people

Must be victims most of the time.

They must leave the house to get burgled

And get beaten up on the street

And they must have their identities stolen

By most of the people they meet.

Now, this amazing statistic

Suggested a plan which seemed sound

Instead of just waiting for some crime to happen

The Police could follow these victims around

And some bright civil servant

Told the Home Sec. just what he could do

(Civil Servants aren't all that poetic,

so for the next line I cannot be too):

"Home Secretary, if you could devise a policy to solve this Repeat Victimisation you could actually significantly reduce the overall level of crime."

I hope and trust you'll believe me

There's no way of making that scan,

But the sad part of this story

Is how it troubled that truly great man,

Who applied the best of his wisdom

And exposed the flaw in the plan:

"This policy can't be adopted -

All the syllables, as you must see,

Will ruin the flow of the soundbite,

So it won't be adopted by me"

And as a poet, I must applaud him:

No scansion and that should be that

But a Home Secretary shouldn't be guided by metre:

You should be reducing the crime rate, you TWAT!

2008

Lord Mandelson and the Plastic Surgeon[1]

Lord Mandelson, as is well known,

Prefers exotic climes

And attends high-powered social gatherings,

Well, on one of those times,

He met a plastic surgeon,

Who put celebs under the knife,

And each discussed the other's work

And the other's life.

The surgeon said "Of course, my work,

is, on the whole, cosmetic;

I make a lesser-known celebrity

Alluring and magnetic.

Underneath they're still the same

I can't add intelligence,

or anything that's alien,

to their personalities, I'm not

that Professor from 'Pygmalion'."

Lord Mandelson, he replied:

"My work was very much the same,

I started as a spin-doctor,

Which is cosmetic surgery

but by another name.

I enhanced a reputation,

Made it seem a man of little talent,

was both visionary and great

and convinced the general public
he was fit to run the state.
Of course, once in Government,
I did less in that line
but I still find my cosmetic services
are required from time to time.
Just like you, of course,
I can only work with the material provided
the visionless see nothing new,
the misguided stay misguided,
but the outward change that I produce
just cannot be derided.
That's the reason why, although,
You know I've been twice-fired,
when it really matters,
I'm still very much demanded and admired."
The cosmetic surgeon he rejoined:
"My work's worth twice of what you do.
You produce one booby at a time;
in my line, I make two."

2008

[1] *For the sake of Lord Mandelson's reputation I should make it clear that this is a work of imagination.*

Bona Headed

"I did it in good faith"
I'm going to say it often
When I grow up to be a man
"I did it in good faith"
Though it doesn't seem to work
On my Mummy or my Nan:
"I did it in good faith"
When I got in a strop
And kicked off my shoe
And "I did it in good faith"
When that vase was broken too.

"I did it in good faith"
Now, if your a politician
"I did it in good faith"
There's no need for an admission
Of any fault on your part,
And no need for contrition:
"I did it in good faith"
When no weapons were found
"I did it in good faith"
When that bank was run into the ground.

Now, I know I'm just a child
And I'm probably quite dense,

But "I did it in good faith"?

Just how does that make sense?

It's the least you should have done,

Not the start of a defence!

If it wasn't done in good faith

You went right beyond the Pale,

It means you lied about those weapons

And the bank was *meant* to fail.

And how would it work

If *everyone*

Could play it by those rules?

Inadequate chief constables

Or the heads of failing schools,

Or all the failing teachers

The government says that we should sack,

If they all messed up in good faith,

Then we'd have to have them back!

And that is why, when I grow up,

It's for Parliament I'm bound,

If you want to lead a blameless life.

It's the only job around.

                                2007-2008

Bounce

It seems the general public

Like the woman in the song

Will cling more tightly to their man

Because he done them wrong

Gordon scuppered the economy

And marched it into bust

Yet now all that has happened

It's in him they place their trust

It seems the public is behaving

Like the classic battered wife

Who should have learned some sense by now

But can see no better life

And so they chose to listen,

And believe him, when

He said that he was sorry

And that he won't do it again

Except he never did say sorry

It was the abuser's other saw

It was someone else's fault

AND DO THEY WANT SOME MORE?

                              2008

Proof

Some things that we know,
We know are the truth
And we know that we know them
Without any proof
But people are fallible,
Memories fail
And when it comes to statistics -
Statistics are hard things
To hit on the nail.
The patterns in nature
Are subtle, you see,
And are not what they seem,
Or may first seem, to be
And even the experts
Aren't always correct
When they say what's coincidence,
Cause and effect.
What is hypothesis,
What's statistically true
In science is the subject
Of the closest review
And that's why I set down
These pondering thoughts
Because it isn't a system
That we use in the Courts

We have expert evidence,
One expert or two,
And one who's not expert,
 A judge[1], forms a view
As to which to accept
And which to reject
Without the learning to judge
Which one is correct.
And in the field of opinion
Or well-studied learning
That may be fine
But when one starts turning
To less studied areas,
Some theoretical flight,
No-one can say
Whether either is right.
And the line is so thin
Between conjecture and fact
That it's frequently passed
Without time to notice,
And still less, react.
And when things go wrong
- And go wrong they do
We all ring our hands
And say "Nobody knew!"

But we all know the problem

And one would have thought

We could think a bit harder

How to treat expert evidence

That's used in court.

                    2008

---

[1] **Footnote:**
Sometimes it's a jury
Has that job to do,
Then twelve unqualified
People decide
What's empiric'lly true,
And as is the way of things
Often are swayed
By factors better deployed
In a beauty parade,
Save it's the grey of the beard
Not the curve of breast
Helps juries decide
Which expert is best.
And here, parenthetic'lly,
I ask you to note
Facts are immune
To the outcome
Of ballot or vote.

Heroic

Now his banner of achievement

Has been modestly unfurled

For the banks, we should give him thanks

But Gordon saved the world!

By what superhuman qualities

Did he achieve this feat?

Perhaps one day soon he'll tell us

And give us all a treat.

Of his speed, no man may speak

But of time travel, speculate:

Now he's transported the economy back

To nineteen seventy-eight.

So let us all show gratitude

Let abuse no more be hurled,

Fighting boom and bust he earned our trust

And Gordon saved the cheerleader

And Gordon saved the World!

                          2008

Be you never so high…

Bombs are not tools of administration

Rockets lack judgment, discrimination.

Rockets and bombs cannot bring peace

They cannot arrest, like the Police,

They cannot with reason, search for the truth,

Cannot be guided by the burden of proof.

They cannot hear evidence put to the test

Convict just the guilty nor acquit the rest.

Rockets and bombs have no gentler guise

They cannot rain justice down from the skies.

"…the law is above you" never meant this.

Bombs are not tools of administration

One cannot, with rockets, rebuild a nation.

                          2009

Perspective or **The Rancid BLT**

The standard of sandwich

        was far short of 'Gold'

The lettuce was wilted

        because it was old,

The bacon looked green,

        not in the sense of unsmoked,

And on the tomato,

        the strong might have choked.

The bread was all right

        although only just

But it leant to the sandwich

        a semi-respectable veneer, or crust

But the sandwiches sold

        without complaint,

        without causing a fight,

Until somebody noticed

        one wasn't cut right

Instead of four quarters,

all perfectly square,

With total congruence

    at every layer,

The filling hung over,

    the slices mis-matched

So back to the counter

    the plate was dispatched

The anger the customer

    felt and expressed

Showed he was very

    much more than distressed

His temples were twitching

    his eyes wild and strange

His general demeanour

    completely deranged

And I don't know what

    so offended his brain

About the cut of the sandwich.

    It's hard to explain

When he'd lived

    with the risk of e-coli,

    salmonella and such

It was the cut of the sandwich

    which offended so much

And then came the row

    about MP's expenses

And I watched the press and the public

    lose all their senses

And it's not that I'm not cross

    and don't want to shout

But there's so much more WORSE

    to get cross about

It's not the expenses,

    so much as the pay

They get for passing bad laws,

    which they do, every day

Without imposing the scrutiny,

    they should impose.

"What does the Bill mean?"

    - well none of them knows

More than what the press-release

    says it will do,

And is that right?

    Well they haven't a clue.

And the person who wrote it

    doesn't care and won't mind

Provided the headlines it gets

    are gen'rally kind.

And more than expenses,

    more than bad legislation

It's the constant lying

    That deserves condemnation:

"For banking I called for

    worldwide regulation."

Not from the Mansion House podium

    you didn't, you said

(And the texts of your speeches

    are there to be read)

The "ingenuity" of our financial markets,

    had ushered in a "Golden age"

You called for "light-touch regulation"

    - That's more worthy of our rage.

When the Commons chamber rang

    to "No more boom and bust"

That's when politicians should

    have completely lost our trust.

When "Prudence" was said to rule

    while spending spiralled higher,

That's when the press and public

    should have spat and shouted "Liar!"

The expenses have cost thousands

    the mismanagement's cost billions

Stolen hopes and dreams and houses,

    pushed unemployment into millions...

But even for these bad things:

    "Apoplexy" and "Revulsion"?

It really is a weakness,

    this modern compulsion,

To condemn immoderately

    without proportion, without sense

That which may only warrant ire,

    given the nature of th'offence.

And I'm left to wonder,

    what worse,

    would we have left to say

Should a Hitler, or Mugabe,

    cross our path one day?

                  May 2009

Riding the Tiger

When a tiger's in a tantrum

You can't explain it has no cause

You simply have to worry

About dodging teeth and claws

When a tiger's in a tantrum

You can't say it shouldn't be

Or stop to list the reasons

For behaving civilly

When a tiger's in a tantrum,

(should you have the knack)

You might find that you are safest,

 When clinging to its back.

It might take you where it wants to go

- over that you'll have no say -

But tantrums cannot last forever

And you will be alive when the tantrum's gone away.

The Public's sometimes like a tiger

And its tantrums can't be beaten

And sometimes a politician must

just try to not get eaten.

But beware the politician,

Who starts to like the ride

Because when it comes to leadership

Tantrums make a rotten guide

Because it isn't really leadership

- but rather is a lack -

To be shouting "Follow me!"

While still on the tiger's back.

                                              June 2009

Poor Law

An American state once could stand it no more -
"Twenty-two-over-seven!" They said Pi should be four
And it's really quite strange what gets passed into law:
Here they're enacting no child can be poor.
As an aim one could do it by handing out cash
But in these straightened times, well that would be rash
So they're not spending money, just passing this law
That says in the future no child shall be poor
And the former-poor-children can ask themselves "What
am I but poor if the law says I'm not?"
For here is the problem, the rub and the sting:
This is a law that doesn't do anything.
For whatever you pass into law and enact
The previously factual doesn't stop being fact.
And while things can be changed, you have to do more
Than grandly announcing you've just passed a law.
And if it were easy, could someone just try
To explain: stopping at children - just tell me why
Their parents aren't covered and single folk too?
If a law's that effective, there's so much more one could do:
Enact no more hunger, enact global bliss -
Or would that seem too much like taking the piss?

                                                                              2009

Staying Put

I'm just going to stick here, immobile as a wall
And I'm not going anywhere,
I'm not going anywhere

And no one's going to shift me, not anyone at all
And I'm not going anywhere,
I'm not going anywhere

Because becoming Labour Leader's the beginning of my dream
And I'm not going anywhere,
I'm not going anywhere

And it is the end of it and all the pieces in-between
And I'm not going anywhere,
I'm not going anywhere

Whoever wants, can leave the Government, I will be here still
And I'm not going anywhere,
I'm not going anywhere

Those women no one's heard of, the bloke that no one ever will,
And I'm not going anywhere,
I'm not going anywhere

The press and commentators may say that I am useless and that I have no vision
But I'm not going anywhere,
I'm not going anywhere

I'm going to cling as long as possible to the fruits of my ambition.
2009

Nursery Rhymes for the Modern World

Hey-diddle-diddle

Hey-diddle-diddle

The cat's on the fiddle

Stagging his shares right over the moon.

The little dog laughed to see such fun

And took profits all afternoon.

Little Bo Peep

Little Bo Peep

Has slaughtered her sheep

To get a slice of the subsidy cake.

She's found she'll get higher yields

By ploughing their fields

And planting acres and acres of rape.

Little Jack Horner

Little Jack Horner

Lost control on a corner,

Test-driving a Ferrari F40.

He ran someone down

But drove on through the town,

Which, children,

Is terribly naughty.

Wee Willie Winkie

Wee Willie Winkie

Runs through the town

Upstairs and downstairs

In his nightgown

Howling at the windows

Barking up the stairs

Another tragic victim

Of 'Community Care'.

Tony Blairy, How Contrary

Tony Blairy, how contrary

To make your party grow

With recycled Tory policies

And spin-doctors all in a row.

The Urban Terrorist

Workers of the world unite,

The middle-class anarchist will tell you what is right.

Having felt the pain of privilege and wealth,

He'll save you from them, by keeping them himself.

END PAGE

www.ingramcontent.com/pod-product-compliance
Ingram Content Group UK Ltd.
Pitfield, Milton Keynes, MK11 3LW, UK
UKHW041435180426
11947UKWH00007B/465